TECHNOLOGY AT WORK

AT THE

FIRE STATION

Louise Spilsbury

Raintree

www.raintreepublishers.co.uk

Visit our website to find out more information about Raintree books.

To order:

☎ Phone 44 (0) 1865 888112

📄 Send a fax to 44 (0) 1865 314091

💻 Visit the Raintree bookshop at www.raintreepublishers.co.uk to browse our catalogue and order online.

Raintree is an imprint of Pearson Education Limited, a company incorporated in England and Wales having its registered office at Edinburgh Gate, Harlow, Essex, CM20 2JE – Registered company number: 00872828

Raintree is a registered trademark of Pearson Education Ltd.

Text © Pearson Education Ltd 2009
First published in hardback in 2009

The moral right of the proprietor has been asserted.

Edited by Louise Galpine and Rachel Howells
Designed by Richard Parker and Tinstar Design Ltd
Original illustrations© Pearson Education Ltd
Illustrations by Darren Lingard
Picture Research by Hannah Taylor and Catherine Bevan
Originated by Modern Age
Printed and bound in China by CTPS

ISBN 978 1 4062 0986 0
13 12 11 10 09
10 9 8 7 6 5 4 3 2 1

British Library Cataloguing in Publication Data
Spilsbury, Louise
  At the fire station. - (Technology at work)
    628.9'25
A full catalogue record for this book is available from the British Library.

Acknowledgements

The publishers would like to thank the following for permission to reproduce photographs: ©Alamy pp. **4** (Danita Delimont), **10**, **18** (Blue Shadows), **12** (Geri Lavrov), **19**, **28 bottom** (Jack Sullivan), **23** (A. T. Willett), **28 middle** (Geri Lavrov); ©BAA Limited p. **24**; ©Corbis/ Mark E. Gibson p. **22**; ©IFEX Technologies p. **25**; ©Photoedit Inc pp. **6** (Dwayne Newton), **27**; ©Photolibrary/ Photodisc/ Skip Nail p. **14**; ©Science Photo Library pp. **16** (Philippe Psaila), **20** (Tony McConnell); ©Total Fire Group Products p. **21**; ©Wishlist Images pp. **5**, **8**, **9**, **13**, **28 top**.

Cover photograph of firefighter directing hose atop ladder, reproduced with permission of ©Corbis (Bill Stormont).

Every effort has been made to contact copyright holders of any material reproduced in this book. Any omissions will be rectified in subsequent printings if notice is given to the publishers.

We would like to thank Ian Graham for his invaluable help in the preparation of this book.

CONTENTS

Some words are printed in bold, **like this**. You can find out what they mean by looking in the glossary.

THE FIRE STATION

You cannot miss a fire station. It is a large building with fire engines inside! There is a lot of space in a fire station for all the equipment that firefighters use in their jobs. Some fire stations have rooms such as a lounge, a kitchen, and bedrooms that firefighters can use while they wait for the next emergency.

Firefighters are trained to know how to put out dangerous fires.

AT WORK

PET RESCUE?

Some people think a firefighter's job includes rescuing cats stuck up trees. Actually, if a cat is healthy it is better to leave it. Rescue attempts often scare cats and make them panic and sometimes fall. You should wait at least 48 hours before calling the fire service to rescue a cat.

What do firefighters do?

Firefighters don't just fight fires! They help out in a range of emergency incidents. These include road accidents, floods, train and aircraft crashes, chemical spills, and bomb explosions. Firefighters use their specialist knowledge and equipment to rescue people who are trapped in burning buildings. They also make sure that other people who are near an incident are kept out of danger.

The large doors on a fire station let huge fire engines in and out quickly.

ALARM CALL!

When someone phones 999 to say there is a fire, workers in a control room send a call to the fire station that is closest to the emergency. A big bell in the station rings and the details and location of the emergency appear on a computer screen. This tells firefighters that there is a fire or that someone needs to be rescued.

Every second counts! Workers in a control room use Internet and telephone technology to send information about a fire to the nearest fire station in an instant.

AT WORK

KEEPING IN TOUCH

Firefighters communicate or keep in touch with each other and other rescue workers to make sure everyone knows what is going on in an emergency. They use radios and also computers. For example, workers at the fire station can send maps of where emergencies are to small computers in the cabs of fire engines.

Detecting smoke

People often know a fire has started when a **smoke detector** starts beeping. Inside there is a small piece of special metal connected to a battery. The metal gives air next to it an electric charge. This completes an **electrical circuit** between two discs. When smoke particles are mixed with the air between the discs the circuit breaks and the alarm goes off.

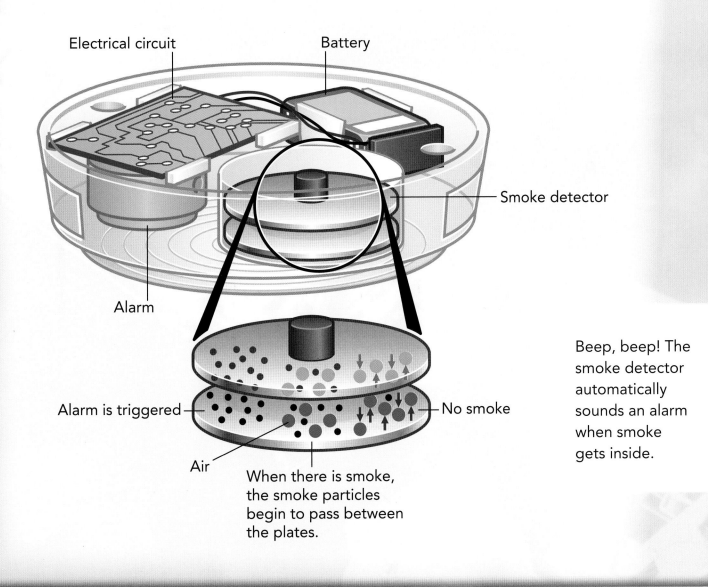

Electrical circuit

Battery

Smoke detector

Alarm

Alarm is triggered

No smoke

Air

When there is smoke, the smoke particles begin to pass between the plates.

Beep, beep! The smoke detector automatically sounds an alarm when smoke gets inside.

A FIREFIGHTER'S SUIT

When the alarm sounds, firefighters immediately pull on their special suits. A firefighter's suit is a uniform that helps protect him or her. It also shows everyone else that they are part of the team dealing with an emergency.

The different parts of this suit work to keep a firefighter safe.

1. Tough, light plastic helmet protects the firefighter's head

2. Thick, waterproof, and fireproof material to protect the firefighter

3. Torch to see in the dark

4. **Velcro™** to seal the jacket quickly and securely

5. **Reflective** stripes reflect light to help the firefighter be seen

6. Thick, waterproof rubber or leather boots protect feet from heat. Steel toe-caps protect toes from falling rubble. Thick soles stop broken glass or nails cutting feet.

Firefighters store helmets above their jackets so they can put both items on quickly.

AT WORK

HOOKS AND EYES

Velcro™ fasteners consist of two strips of nylon. One has tiny hooks on it, and the other has mini loops called eyes. Pressing the strips together makes the hooks catch on the eyes. Each hook and eye is quite weak, but many working together create a strong grip.

KEEP BREATHING

Fires can produce choking smoke and very hot or poisonous gases. If firefighters breathe this in it can choke them, so they take their own air supply. Firefighters wear a Self Contained Breathing Apparatus or SCBA. This is a tank of clean air with a tube leading to a mask that fits around the mouth and nose.

IN THE FUTURE

Scientists are developing robot snakes that can slither into burning buildings. They are fitted with **sensors** to find the hottest part of the fire and spray water onto it!

Firefighters have enough air in their SCBA to last for about 45 minutes.

The **pressure gauge** shows the pressure or push of air in their tank. When the pressure drops, it means the air is running out.

The different parts of a firefighter's breathing apparatus all have a different job to do to make it work.

The air inside is **compressed**, which means it is squashed to fit more in a smaller space.

The SCBA tank is made of light aluminium metal. It is covered in a material that **insulates** the tank. That means it stops heat passing into the tank and making the gas hot.

A regulator is a special valve (flap) that makes sure air does not blow too fast into the breathing mask.

THE FIRE ENGINE

Fire engines are big trucks that transport firefighters, water, and equipment to the scene of a fire or other emergency. Most have a large cab to carry up to eight firefighters. The fire engine carries ladders on the top. On the sides there are **lockers** with pull-down doors that store tools and other equipment.

Fire engines are specially designed with lots of different equipment and lockers to hold more tools. Firefighters have to remember where it all is!

AT WORK

GET A GRIP!

Fire engines drive to fires even when roads are icy so some have snow chains. By each tyre there is a small rubber disc with chains attached. The discs are lowered so they rub against the moving tyres. The fire engine does not skid because the chains move round and land between the tyre and the ground.

Being seen and heard

Fire engines move fast to emergencies so they have to warn people to get out of the way. They are painted bright red or yellow in **reflective** paint and have flashing blue or red lights to make sure they can be seen. Fire engines also have **sirens** that make a range of noises. They might use a wailing noise on a clear road or a shorter warning 'yelp' to clear busy traffic away.

Firefighters turn on sirens in a fire engine to protect themselves and other road users.

LIFTING HIGHER

When people are trapped in tall buildings, normal ladders are not long enough so firefighters use a **turntable ladder**. This is a very long ladder that sits on the back of a fire engine.

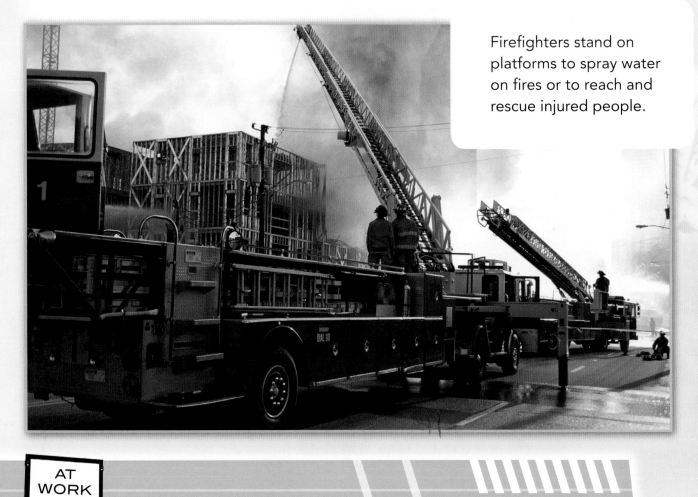

Firefighters stand on platforms to spray water on fires or to reach and rescue injured people.

AT WORK

GROWING LEGS

The top end of a ladder can get so heavy that it could make the fire engine topple over. Fire engines stop this by using four legs called stabilizers. These extend out to give the engine a wider base.

The turntable ladder has three sliding sections that stretch as much as 50 metres (165 feet) into the air. The ladder twists on the turntable so it can turn in all directions. Some turntable ladders have a metal **platform** at the end which firefighters can stand on.

Liquid power

Firefighters move the ladder using a few buttons. These buttons operate **pumps** that push oil through long, narrow pipes. The pipes lead to both ends of short, wide cylindrical (tube-shaped) **rams**. The liquid pushes a **piston** in the ram. The ram extends or gets shorter depending on which end the oil moves into. When liquid is used to do work we call it a **hydraulic** machine.

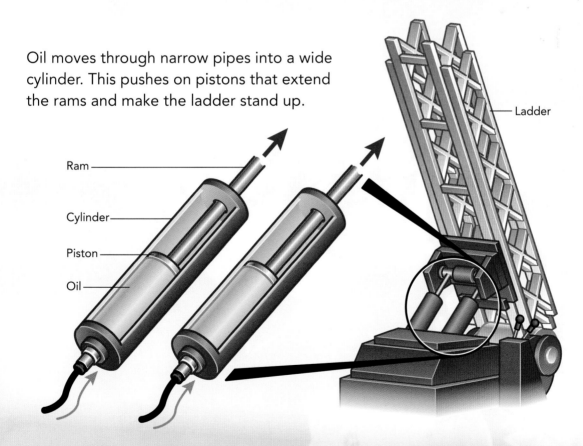

Oil moves through narrow pipes into a wide cylinder. This pushes on pistons that extend the rams and make the ladder stand up.

Ladder

Ram

Cylinder

Piston

Oil

PUTTING OUT FIRES

Three things combine to cause a fire: **fuel**, **oxygen**, and heat. Fuel is the thing which burns, for example, wood or oil. Oxygen is a gas in the air. Heat can come from a match or a spark from faulty electrical equipment.

To put out a fire, firefighters remove or block one of these three things. They spray cold water on fires to lower the heat. They spray foam or powder to stop oxygen getting to the fuel. They knock down parts of buildings, such as the roof, to remove fuel and stop a fire spreading.

Firefighters have to hold tight to large hoses because water sprays out so quickly and forcefully.

AT WORK

EXTREME SPRAYING

Fire engines have giant water tanks and **pumps** that can spray water over 100 metres (300 feet) from hoses. When they run out of water, firefighters get water from **hydrants** built into city streets, or from any nearby water source, such as rivers. They even use swimming pools sometimes!

How fire extinguishers work

Firefighters often use fire extinguishers to put out small fires. Fire extinguishers work by using the force of gas pressure. Pressing the handle releases carbon dioxide from a canister. This gas pushes down on liquid in a tank. The foam then shoots out of the tube and onto the flames.

4 The foam shoots out of the extinguisher through a nozzle at the top of the tube.

1 Squeezing the handle releases carbon dioxide gas inside the fire extinguisher.

2 This makes gas pressure in the confined space. The gas pushes down on the foam in the tank.

Fire extinguishers prevent small fires from growing. Gas pressure in the tank forces the foam out.

3 The pressure forces the foam up a tube.

IN THE LOCKERS

The **lockers** on a fire engine contain a giant toolkit for firefighters. Some lockers contain long lengths of coiled-up hoses. Others have hand tools such as axes for smashing down doors and hooked pikes for pulling down ceilings to reach fires. Other tools help to cut or prise open wrecked cars so people trapped inside can escape.

The long axe handle increases the force the firefighter uses to smash the axehead into the roof.

AT WORK

WEDGE IT OPEN

An axehead is a simple machine called a **wedge**. Wedges convert a small downwards force into a greater force sideways. The sharp axe blade goes into wood and splits it apart.

Spreaders and cutters

Jaws of life are powerful machines with jaws that can slice through metal or spread wide to force metal apart. The jaws are connected like pliers. They are a type of simple machine made of two **levers** joined at a **pivot**. The jaws are powered by **rams**. The **piston** moves the pivot up or down to move the levers further apart or closer together.

Ram power! The firefighter slides a switch to move the piston one way to open and the other to shut the jaws.

SEEING THROUGH SMOKE

Burning buildings are usually full of thick black smoke so, to help find their way around, firefighters use thermal imaging cameras. These detect differences in **infrared** heat in front of them. They help firefighters find survivors in the dark because people give off heat.

In this thermal image of a saucepan, hotter parts are lighter than cooler parts.

AT WORK

DIFFERENT RAYS

Infrared is a type of light we cannot normally see. It is made by anything that produces heat. The hotter something is, the more infrared is produced. Unlike light we can see, infrared passes easily through smoke.

How thermal imaging cameras work

Infrared heat moves into the camera onto a **sensor**. This is made up of small squares, and each square heats up a different amount depending on how much infrared hits it. More electricity flows through hotter squares and less through colder ones.

A mini computer turns the electrical information from the sensor into an image on the screen. The computer makes a new image many times a second, so the firefighter sees a moving image.

Sensor — Mini computer

Helmets can be high-tech. This helmet features thermal imaging technology.

Infrared radiation

Eyepiece —

This thermal imaging camera is mounted on the firefighter's helmet and the screen is in a fold-down eyepiece.

SPECIAL INCIDENTS

If a lorry crashes and spills dangerous chemicals on the road, firefighters are part of the emergency team that deals with the clear up. They always wear **hazmat suits** when clearing up harmful substances. These suits are a bit like all-over rubber gloves! They are made of two layers of rubber with a tough fibre layer in between so they cannot rip. The suit fits over a firefighter who is wearing a breathing apparatus.

Hazmat suits like these protect firefighters from dangerous materials or substances.

Aeroplanes can get to the main areas of a forest fire swiftly and drop fire-retardant chemicals directly onto the flames.

IN THE FUTURE

Airships, like enormous balloons, may one day be able to transport enough water to fill an Olympic swimming pool high above forest fires and drench the flames below!

Wildfires

Wildfires are large fires that can spread quickly through woodland or grassland over a wide area. Firefighters hit burning grass with fire flappers shaped rather like paddles to cut the **oxygen** supply to the fire. They stop fires from spreading by removing plant **fuel**. Firefighters clear areas using axes and digging tools. They often use helicopters and aeroplanes to dump water or powder onto forest fires from above. Some flying machines have to land to refill their tanks, but others can fly over lakes and scoop up water!

EXTREME HEAT

Fires at airports and petrol stations are some of the hottest fires. This is because there is lots of oil and other **fuels** to keep fires burning fast and furious. The extreme heat can damage normal fire engines and injure firefighters if they get too close. So they use special equipment to put out these dangerous fires.

Firefighters brave extremely hot flames from burning fuel tanks to put out an aeroplane that is on fire.

AT WORK

EXPLOSIVE CARGO

Firefighters have to put out airport fires especially quickly. This is because aircraft usually carry lots of fuel so they can fly long distances. When fires spread on aircraft, the fuel can explode. This would kill passengers, crew, and firefighters and cause a lot of damage.

Special engines

Some airport fire engines have **hydraulic** arms on top that can spray foam in a fine mist onto aircraft fires from above. The arm sometimes has a sharp point called a snozzle that can push into the aircraft and put out fires inside. Firefighting tanks have a powerful foam sprayer instead of a gun on top. The thick metal tank body protects the firefighters inside. These tanks stay cool by spraying water on themselves!

Firefighting tanks can withstand any extreme fire.

After they return to the fire station, firefighters get ready for the next emergency! They clean dirt and smoke off their equipment and make sure it is working properly. For example, the firefighters oil the moving parts in the **jaws of life**. They check the fire engines are topped up with water and fuel.

Firefighters also make visits to schools and offices to teach people about fire safety. For example, they encourage people to buy fire alarms. Firefighters also visit buildings such as old people's homes or firework factories to make sure they are doing all they can to prevent fires.

Training

Firefighters do lots of training so they can deal with any emergency quickly and safely. In the yard by the station there is often a tall concrete tower and old cars that firefighters set alight! Then they practise using firefighting equipment such as thermal imaging cameras.

AT WORK

IN THE GYM

Some fire stations have their own gym! Firefighters do exercises to get stronger and fitter so they can do their job well. After all, they never know when they might have to carry injured people from burning buildings and break down doors.

Some fire stations have empty houses in their yards so that firefighters can practise rescuing people from different levels of a building.

FIRE TECHNOLOGY

Insulating materials

Stop heat from passing through by:

- stopping heat passing through a firefighter's suit and boots

- stopping heat from conducting around an SCBA airtank

Pumps

Pumps push water through thin tubes to make it shoot out of hoses on the:

- fire engine

- firefighting tank

Hydraulic rams

Create large pushes in enclosed spaces using liquid **pressure** to:

- lift and extend long, heavy **turntable ladder**

- cut tough materials with **jaws of life**

Compressed gas

Creates large pushes in enclosed spaces using gas pressure to:

- force out water, foam, or powder from a fire extinguisher

- fit more air in a tank and push it out fast to a firefighter's mouth and nose in an SCBA

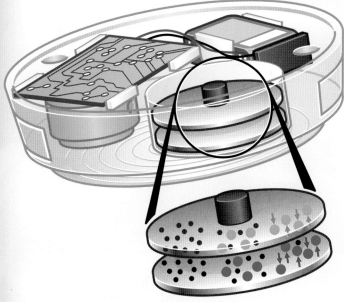

Sensors

Parts that detect light, heat, changes in electric current, or pressure in order to control machines. They:

- sense smoke to make alarm go off in a **smoke detector**

- sense **infrared** light in a thermal imaging camera

GLOSSARY

compressed pushed into a small space. Air is compressed into tanks.

electrical circuit path through which electricity flows. Electrical machines such as light bulbs and pumps stop working when electrical circuits are broken or switched off.

fuel substance that creates heat when it is burnt

gauge measuring instrument. A pressure gauge shows how much a gas or liquid pushes.

hazmat suit rubber and plastic clothing that protects people from harmful chemicals and other hazardous material

hydrant source of water in urban areas

hydraulic machine that is operated by pushing water or oil through a pipe

infrared invisible light we can feel as heat

insulate protect from heat

jaws of life machine that uses hydraulic power to cut or prise open metal

lever simple machine that helps us do more work. An axe handle is a type of lever.

locker storage compartment for putting things such as tools safely inside

oxygen type of gas found in air that we need to breathe

piston cylindrical piece of metal that liquid moves up and down inside a ram

pivot short piece that supports other pieces that turn about it. There is a pivot between the two sides of a pair of scissors.

platform raised flat surface. Firefighters can work from the platform on a turntable ladder.

pressure push on a surface

pump machine that creates high gas or liquid pressure. Pumps make water spray from hoses.

ram device that uses the push of liquid to do work. In a turntable ladder, a ram makes the ladder move up and down.

reflective surface that sends light or heat bouncing off it

sensor device that senses light or other signals and produces an electronic signal from them

siren warning signal of loud noise. Emergency vehicles such as fire engines and ambulances all use sirens.

smoke detector device to detect smoke and warn people that a fire has started. Many people have several smoke detectors to make their homes safe.

turntable ladder long ladder on top of a fire engine

Velcro™ fastener made of strips of nylon that stick together

wedge triangular shaped simple machine that can be used to force things apart. Blades on axes and knives are types of wedges.

FIND OUT MORE

Books

Blazing Bush and Forest Fires (Awesome Forces of Nature), Louise and
   Richard Spilsbury (Heinemann Library, 2003)

Emergency Vehicles (Transport Around the World), Chris Oxlade
   (Heinemann Library, 2002)

Firefighter (High Interest Books), Philip Abraham (Children's Press, 2003)

Firefighter (People Who Help Us), Rebecca Hunter (Cherrytree Books, 2005)

Websites

www.firefightercentral.com/firefighter_history.htm
Visit this site to learn about the history of firefighting. Find out how today's
firefighting technology is very different from in the past.

www.firekills.gov.uk
For information about cooking safety, electrical safety, and tackling fires in
the home, visit this site.

www.smokeybear.com/fighting.asp
On this website you can learn about how wildfires start, how people put them
out and lots of other interesting information.

INDEX